African Twist

Maggie Ogunbanwo

Photography Huw Jones

African Twist

Maggie Ogunbanwo
Photography Huw Jones

For Sage Todz, my vegan inspiration.

GRAFFEG

Contents

Starters & Soups

1. Golden Rice with Raisins   12

2. Lemon Mushrooms   16

3. Aubergine and Tomato Caviar   20

4. Chilli-Flavoured Couscous
   with Grilled Vegetables   24

5. Creamy Brussels Sprouts Soup   30

6. Carrot and Apricot Soup   34

7. Two Colour Mash   38

8. Coconut Rice with Papaya/
   Pawpaw   42

9. Cucumber Salad with
   Nigella Seeds   46

10. Bakes/Buns   50

Mains

11. Vegetable Pirate Stew   56

12. Kale and Onion Stir-Fried   60

13. Walnut and Pomegranate Stew   64

14. Maggie's Persian Seasoning   68

15. Green Banana/Plantain Curry   72

16. Three Bean and Coconut Curry   76

17. Pan-Fried Cauliflower with
    Ginger and Coriander   80

18. Stir-Fried Broccoli   84

19. Sweet Potato with Peanut
    Butter Stew   88

20. Courgette, Kale and Leek
    Bitetuteku   92

21. Green Bean Casserole   96

Cover photo: Rum Caramel Oranges
© Huw Jones, recipe page 106.

Desserts

22. Banfora: Burkina Welsh Cakes 102

23. Rum Caramel Oranges 106

24. Chin Chin 110

25. Clementines in Port 114

26. Plantain Loaf 118

27. Puff-puff with Kombucha 122

Party Favourites

28. Ginger Spritzer with Pineapple 130

29. Chickpea Dip 132

30. Tomato Dip 136

31. Aubergine Dip 140

Maggie Ogunbanwo 144

Acknowledgements 147

Introduction

The vast continent of Africa offers up an equally vast range of food possibilities and combinations, from the added heat of chillies in West Africa and sweet and savoury flavour combinations in North African cooking to leafy greens and pulses from East Africa and the mix of Asian flavours in Southern African dishes.

My experience of African cooking led me to the conclusion that most meals are vegetarian or vegan by nature and then protein is added in one form or another. With the trend towards plant-based meals gaining popularity, it seems only right to share some African-inspired recipes to showcase that, with just a little bit of this 'n' that, any plant-based offering can be imbued with an African twist.

I have grown up around or prepared several of the recipes myself, from puff-puff, the scent always accompanied by memories of my Nana, to green banana curry that speaks of my mixed African heritage. You see, in Nigeria I would be looked at strangely by western Nigerians when preparing green banana curry, as this came down through my Cameroonian heritage. The reaction to peanut soup the first time I prepared it for my Yoruba mum-in-law was also an eye-opener to me – I thought everyone enjoyed a good groundnut/peanut stew.

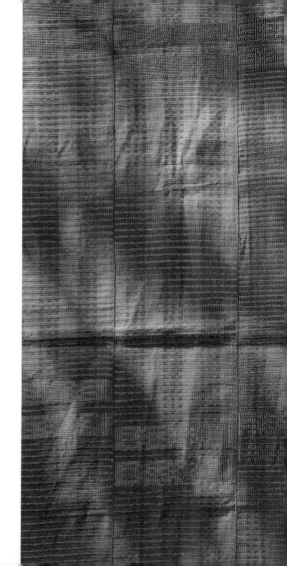

Each recipe in this collection has the Maggie's African Twist touch, either through the addition of herbs and spices or the infusion of chilli, and seeks to gently introduce the variety of African cooking available to enhance your everyday dish.

Maggie Ogunbanwo

Additional Information

Curry

The curry spice might just be the most travelled of all spices – this veritable globetrotter is found in far-flung corners. Maggie's Curry lights the hard-to-reach taste buds and teases them to life. The delight that this blend of flavours curates with diverse dishes is only as limited as your imagination! Rejuvenate your dishes and palate with this authentic curry spice created just for you.

Jerk

As a staple that calls to mind the musical lilt of island natives, ocean breezes and the metallic twang of the signature steel pans of its music, jerk is the lifeblood of Caribbean cuisine and has its roots in African spicing. Our jerk spice treats all food cooked in it and deposits a chequered blend of savoury goodness with each morsel.

Naija This & That Seasoning

I closed my eyes and was transported back to a sunny kitchen, light streaming in through every louvre and smells wafting up to the ceiling. 'A little bit of this and that,' some of the other mothers said, creating amazing smells and flavours.

I opened my eyes and added a mix of three spices and lo and behold I had recreated flavours, tastes and promises of home in another land.

And so was born the Naija This & That mix, used as an addition while cooking vegetable dishes, roast potatoes... In other words, mama's all-purpose seasoning.

Some of these recipes can be served together as a colourful vegan bowl or platter: buns, aubergine caviar, kale stir-fry, chickpea and spinach fritters and lemon mushrooms will make a beautiful, tasty, colourful combination.

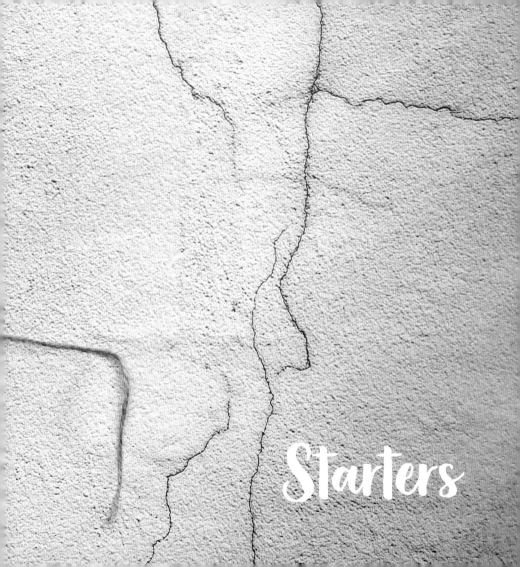

Starters

Golden Rice with Raisins

Golden Rice with Raisins

Serves 4 | Prep time 5 minutes | Cook time 15 minutes

Ingredients

250g long-grain rice

500ml water

1 teaspoon olive oil

2 pieces cinnamon bark

4 green cardamoms
(whole)

1 teaspoon turmeric
powder

1 teaspoon paprika

1 teaspoon salt

100g raisins

Method

· After following the instructions on the packet, place
the rice in a medium-sized saucepan or in the bowl of
a rice cooker.

· Add the water, olive oil and all the rest of the
ingredients to the rice and give it a brief stir to mix
everything evenly.

· If using a saucepan, turn the heat up to high and
bring the contents to a rolling boil.

· Turn down the heat as low as possible, cover the pan
with a lid and simmer the contents for 12-15 minutes,
until the water has dried up and the rice is soft to the
taste.

· If using a rice cooker, place the lid on and allow to
cook. It will switch itself off or to warm when ready.

· Serve hot.

The rice can be cooled and used as the basis for a salad. If using another type of rice e.g. basmati or Thai jasmine rice, the cooking time will vary.

Some rice instructions require a prewash before cooking; if this is the case, follow the instructions and drain well using a colander or fine sieve before bringing to the boil.

Inspired by South African Malay cooking, this is a fragrant, golden rice that adds beautiful colour to any meal. Serve with a mixed bean and coconut curry or other curry of your choice.

Lemon Mushrooms

Lemon Mushrooms

Serves 4 | Prep time 8-10 minutes | Cook time 4-5 minutes

Ingredients

500g mushrooms
(shitake, oyster and
similarly firm varieties
are best)

1 large or 2 small lemons
(juice only)

2 tablespoons olive oil

Sprinkling of black
pepper

Method

· Slice all the mushrooms thickly.

· Juice the lemons.

· Place a wide pan or frying pan over high heat and
add the olive oil.

· When hot, turn the heat down before adding all the
chopped mushrooms to the pan.

· Add the lemon juice, salt and a sprinkling of black
pepper and stir-fry the mushrooms until they are
cooked through, about 4-5 minutes. Serve hot.

At Maggie's we travelled around Africa through a series of pop-up restaurants, bringing Africa to Penygroes by food. We discovered this delightful recipe and took advantage of the wide variety of mushrooms available to create this dish. A level of tartness that mixes with the different textures of the various mushrooms gives you this quick gluten and dairy-free recipe. It would typically be seasoned with salt and a lot of hot chilli sauce.

Aubergine and Tomato Caviar

Aubergine and Tomato Caviar

Serves 6 | Prep time 10 minutes | Cook time 60 minutes

Ingredients

2 aubergines

2 tablespoons olive oil

1 onion, finely chopped

1 tablespoon tomato puree

1 teaspoon salt

1 teaspoon Naija This & That Spice

4 tablespoons freshly chopped coriander or parsley

Freshly ground black pepper

Lemon wedges and mixed salad leaves to garnish

Method

· Preheat the oven to 190°C/375°F/Gas 5. Prick the skin of the aubergines all over, place directly onto the oven rack towards the top of the oven and roast for 40 minutes, turning once halfway through.

· Remove from the oven and allow to cool.

· When the aubergines are cool enough, peel away the stalks and chop the flesh until a soft puree is obtained.

· Heat the oil in a small frying pan and sauté the onion over low heat for about 10 minutes until soft and golden.

· Stir in the tomato puree, salt, Naija This and That Spice and aubergine puree. Continue to cook over high heat for 2 minutes to remove excess moisture in the aubergine, stirring all the time. Remove from the heat and allow to cool completely.

- Transfer the caviar to a mixing bowl and stir in the coriander or parsley.

- Serve on a bed of mixed salad leaves garnished with a wedge of lemon.

They say that caviar is 'food of the gods'.
Well, this is the vegan food of the gods.
Soft, fleshy baked aubergines team with onions,
tomatoes and spice to give you a delectable side
dish, or a main when served with a salad.

Chilli-Flavoured Couscous with Grilled Vegetables

Chilli-Flavoured Couscous with Grilled Vegetables

Serves 4 | Prep time 10-12 minutes | Cook time 20 minutes

Ingredients

2 aubergines, cut into 5mm slices and cut in half again lengthways

2 red onions, peeled and cut into 8 wedges

2 red peppers, cored, seeded and cut into 8 strips

4 plum tomatoes, seeded and quartered

12 closed-cup mushrooms, cut into thick slices

7 tablespoons olive oil

1 teaspoon salt

1 tablespoon chilli and garlic oil (plus optional extra for serving)

250g couscous

4 tablespoons vegetable stock (optional)

Freshly chopped parsley (to serve)

Method

· Preheat the grill to high. On a large baking tray, arrange all the vegetables in a single layer. Drizzle with chilli and garlic oil and season with salt.

· Place under the grill on the highest shelf and cook for 5 minutes, then turn the vegetables over. Cook for

After a stint working with an Italian, I tend to grill my seasoned vegetables in the oven at 200°C and this could work here. Quinoa grains would make a nice substitute and are commonly used in some parts of African cooking.

a further 5 minutes and turn the vegetables again. (Keep the vegetables under the grill on a low heat while you prepare the couscous.)

· Put 250ml water in a large saucepan with the chilli and garlic oil and teaspoon of salt. Bring to a gentle simmer then stir in the couscous.

· Cover, remove from the heat and leave for 3 minutes. Fluff up the grains with a fork and keep warm over a very low heat.

· Turn the grill back up to high and cook the vegetables for 5 more minutes until they are well charred and hot.

Chilli-Flavoured Couscous with Grilled Vegetables

- To serve, divide the couscous between four plates. Spoon the vegetables over the couscous, drizzle over any cooking juices and moisten with vegetable stock if you like.

- Sprinkle with parsley and add a few extra drops of chilli and garlic oil just before serving if you wish.

I spent some of my early years in the north of Nigeria, where couscous is a staple food, but did not get to try couscous until I lived in Brixton with a group of hippie friends. Further travels to Morocco showed me how versatile couscous is, served as a main or used in desserts. It is a quick, easy, go-to food and leftovers are excellent in salads.

Creamy Brussels Sprouts Soup

Creamy Brussels Sprouts Soup

Serves 6 | Prep time 20 minutes | Cook time 30 minutes

Ingredients

50ml olive oil

450g Brussels sprouts
(trimmed and halved)

1 medium onion, chopped

25g plain flour

450ml vegetable stock

Freshly grated nutmeg

150ml plant-based milk

½ teaspoon grains of
paradise

Salt

Maggie's Green Chilli
Sauce

To garnish:

Flaked almonds, grated
nutmeg, brussels sprout
leaves

Method

· Heat the olive oil in a large saucepan and stir-fry the
  sprouts and onions for 5-6 minutes until just tender.

· Remove and reserve a few sprout leaves for the
  garnish.

· Stir in the flour and cook over a medium heat for
  1 minute.

· Gradually add the stock, beating with a whisk until
  smooth. Bring to the boil and reduce the heat, then
  cover and simmer for 15-20 minutes. Add seasoning
  to taste – this could be salt and a touch of Maggie's
  Green Chilli Sauce.

My first experience of Brussels sprouts was at Christmas time when I first moved to the UK. I was fascinated at the way locals prepared them removing a lot of the outer leaves and adding the cross at the stalk end. I was equally as fascinated at the number of debates around these mini 'cabbagy' looking veg. In our café we would use any leftover brussels sprouts to make this thick, delightful and, dare I say, spicy soup.

- Process until smooth. Reheat gently (do not boil), then stir in the milk.

- Serve hot and garnish with flaked almonds, grated nutmeg, a spinkling of Guinea pepper/grains of paradise and reserved Brussels sprout leaves. (A sprinkling of grains of paradise adds that African twist.)

Carrot and Apricot Soup

Carrot and Apricot Soup

Serves 6 | Prep time 5 minutes | Cook time 35 minutes

Ingredients

50ml vegetable oil

1 onion, chopped

600g carrots, sliced

1.1L vegetable stock

1 x (400g) can apricots or mango in natural juice

Sherry or mead

4 teaspoons snipped chives

Salt and pepper to taste

To garnish:

Soya cream

Method

· Heat the oil in a large saucepan and fry the chopped onions and sliced carrots over a low heat for 5 minutes, stirring frequently.

· Add the stock, bring to the boil, then reduce the heat and simmer for 15-20 minutes until the carrots are soft.

· Put the stock mixture plus the apricots or mangos and their juice into a blender and process until smooth.

· Return to the pan and add the sherry or mead, chives, salt and pepper to taste.

· Heat the soup, stirring frequently, but do not allow to boil. Garnish with swirls of soya cream.

Soups are full of goodness and health-supporting plant-based properties. In this recipe the apricots enhance the taste of the carrots giving a vibrant, tasty, tangy and thick soup that can be served with buns/bakes or flatbread. Mangos may be used in place of the apricots to mix things up. At Maggie's we make our own vegetable stock from a mix of infused vegetables and water. If you use a shop-bought stock, please check it is suitable for vegans.

Two Colour Mash

Two Colour Mash

Serves 4 | Prep time 7 minutes | Cook time 25 minutes

Ingredients

450g parsnips, peeled and roughly chopped

450g carrots, peeled and thinly sliced

30ml soya/plant-based milk of choice

Salt and black pepper to taste

Grated nutmeg

Method

· Place the carrots and parsnips in two separate saucepans with enough water to cover.

· Add a pinch of salt and cook for 15-20 minutes over a medium heat until tender.

· Set aside 60ml of the liquid from the parsnips, then drain both saucepans and set aside.

· Place the vegetables in a food processor with the liquid and milk.

· Process until almost smooth, retaining some texture – this could be done using a potato masher.

· Add salt, pepper and nutmeg to taste. Serve hot.

Sweet potato could be used in
place of carrots or parsnips.

Coconut Rice with Papaya/Pawpaw

Coconut Rice with Papaya/Pawpaw

Serves 4 | Prep time 15-20 minutes | Cook time 15-20 minutes

Ingredients

200g long-grain rice

½ teaspoon salt

½ teaspoon cinnamon

500ml coconut milk (or 250ml coconut milk and 250ml water)

Dried pawpaw pieces

1 teaspoon paprika

Method

· Add the rice, salt, cinnamon, paprika and coconut milk to a saucepan over high heat.

· Stir and bring the contents of the pan to the boil, then turn down the heat to low and simmer for about 12 minutes.

· Stir in the papaya/pawpaw pieces and let the rice cook and dry out for a further 2 to 3 minutes.

· Serve with my vegetable pirate stew or other stew of choice and enjoy.

Cold left over rice can be used as the basis for a salad.

If you dropped the seeds of papaya, which I always knew as pawpaw as a child, the next week or so there would be a pawpaw plant sprouting up. At least that was how it appeared to me as a child. Pawpaw was prolific in my childhood recollections and every compound seemed to have a least one tree growing.

I recall the first time I observed the preparation of coconut rice by my aunty. It took hours as she went through the painful process of breaking coconuts, grating them and putting them through water and a sieve to extract more of the liquid. I was so pleased when I discovered coconut cream in a block and even more so when canned coconut milk became readily available on UK shop shelves.

Ripe pawpaw would be the go-to fruit for afters during the growing season and I discovered a use for unripe pawpaw/papaya on my travels in Thailand. It also makes a fab soup in Tanzanian cooking.

In this recipe the dried pawpaw/papaya serves to add a bit of colour and texture to the dish.

Cucumber Salad with Nigella Seeds

Cucumber Salad with Nigella Seeds

Serves 2-3 | Prep time 40 minutes

Ingredients

½ cucumber

Salt

1 fresh green chilli, seeded and finely chopped

½ small red chilli, seeded and finely chopped

½ teaspoon nigella/onion seeds

3 teaspoons white wine vinegar

½ teaspoon sugar

Method

· Slice the cucumber very thinly (or chop into squares).

· Place cucumber slices/squares in a colander and sprinkle with plenty of salt. Leave to drain for 30 minutes, then rinse thoroughly under cold running water.

· Pat dry with kitchen paper and arrange on a serving plate.

· In a bowl, mix the chopped red and green chillies with the onion seeds, white wine vinegar and sugar and set aside.

· Before serving, pour the chilli mix over the cucumbers. Serve as a side salad.

Tip: Toast the onion seeds for a few minutes in a dry frying pan then cool before use.

In Morocco they use nigella/onion seeds as a remedy to clear blocked nostrils. Tied in a piece of muslin and rubbed vigorously, it produces a strong scent that when inhaled will work as a vapour rub. In this recipe it is mixed with chillies to create a tasty, colourful side that is tempting to the eyes and the taste buds. I pay tribute to the late Bob Munroe, a South African friend in whose home I first experienced this combination.

Bakes/Buns

Bakes/Buns

Makes 12-15 | Prep time 20 minutes | Cook time 10-20 minutes

Ingredients

450g plain flour

2 tablespoons vegetable oil

½ teaspoon salt

2 teaspoons baking powder

2 teaspoons caster sugar

250-260ml soya or other plant-based milk

Method

- Sift the dry ingredients into a bowl, then add in the oil until the mixture resembles breadcrumbs.

- Pour in the milk and stir to make a soft dough.

- Knead the dough for 5 minutes, then chill for 10-20 minutes.

- Divide the dough into plum-sized pieces, roll into balls, then flatten in the palms of your hands to 1cm thickness.

- Shallow fry in hot oil until golden brown on both sides: about 2 minutes on one side, and 1 minute on the reverse side.

- Serve as a side with curry, soup or eat at breakfast time with spiced tea.

As street food, breakfast or a stomach-filler, these are housed in see-through wood and glass boxes and hawked from morning until they are all sold out, balanced securely on the head of those calling out, 'Buns, buy your buns.'

Mains

Vegetable Pirate Stew

Vegetable Pirate Stew

Serves 8 | Prep time 2-8 minutes | Cook time 30 minutes

Ingredients

1 medium onion

2 cloves garlic

1-2 teaspoons Maggie's Original Chilli Sauce

1 small red bell pepper, roughly chopped

5ml ginger powder

30ml molasses/golden syrup (or 35g dates/raisins, mashed)

100ml vegetable oil

120ml vegetable stock

120ml coconut milk

300g frozen mixed vegetables

2-3 teaspoons Maggie's African Twist Pirate Stew Mix

Method

· Blend the onion, garlic, bell pepper and ginger together in a food processor or blender to a smooth paste with a little water.

· In a medium saucepan, add the oil, pour in the processed mixture and stir-fry on high for 2-3 minutes.

· Add the stock, coconut milk, molasses/syrup or date mash, Pirate Stew spice mix and vegetables and cook gently until the vegetables are cooked through.

· Adjust salt and chilli to taste and serve with boiled rice and fried plantains.

Kale and Onion Stir-Fried

Kale and Onion Stir-Fried

Serves 6 | Prep time 4-6 minutes | Cook time 8-10 minutes

Ingredients

250g kale

3 tablespoons olive oil

2 large shallots, very finely chopped

2 garlic cloves, crushed

1-3 teaspoons Maggie's African Twist Green Chilli Sauce

Salt, to taste

Method

· Wash the kale under cold running water.

· Cut out the tough stalks and discard.

· Taking five or six leaves at a time, roll them up tightly like a cigar.

· Using a sharp vegetable knife, slice the kale as finely as possible.

· Heat the oil in a saucepan over medium heat, then stir-fry the shallots and garlic for 1-2 minutes.

· Add the shredded kale to the shallots and garlic and stir-fry over high heat for about 5 minutes until the kale starts to soften but is still crisp. Serve hot.

A few years back I discovered cavolo nero or black kale, and it would work well in this recipe. A huge variety of green vegetables/leaves are used in African cooking, from simple chop and stir-fry to elaborate sauces like egusi soup!

Kale is one of the vegetables found in the UK that can reproduce some of the qualities of African vegetables and very often people are not sure what to do with it. This simple recipe will help you enjoy the versatile vegetable that is kale.

Walnut and Pomegranate Stew

Walnut and Pomegranate Stew

Serves 4 | Prep time 15 minutes | Cook time 20 minutes

Ingredients

300g dried walnuts, finely crushed

4 tablespoons pomegranate paste

3-4 teaspoons sugar

2 medium onions, processed to a paste

2 tablespoons vegetable oil

1½ teaspoons tomato puree

1-2 teaspoons Maggie's Persian Seasoning

Salt and guinea pepper to taste

Method

· Place the oil in a medium saucepan over high heat, when hot add the processed onions and stir fry for 2 minutes.

· Add the finely crushed walnuts, sugar, pomegranate paste, tomato puree, Maggie's Persian Seasoning and 450ml of vegan stock or water.

· Cook for 20 minutes until the flavours combine and the stew thickens. Adjust the seasoning to taste and serve with two colour mash and plain boiled Malawi Kilombero rice.

You can find pomegranate paste also sold as pomegranate molasses in ethnic food shops or online.

A chance find during one of my creative periods had me trying out and loving this recipe and how the walnuts, pomegranate paste and seasoning work to create such a delightfully flavoured sauce. The African twist comes from the fact that we have several curry-type stews that we prepare and then add protein to before serving, but here I have modified this recipe to just the sauce, to which you can add vegetables of choice. Cooked pumpkin or squash would make a really nice addition before heating through and serving with golden rice with raisins or plain boiled Malawi Kilombero rice.

Maggie's Persian Seasoning

Maggie's Persian Seasoning

Makes 230g | Cook time 3 minutes

Ingredients

120g coriander seeds

120g cinnamon

60g cumin

45g black pepper

30g cardamom seeds

30g whole cloves

30g dried chillies

75g turmeric

Method

· Dry fry all the whole ingredients in a large frying pan over high heat for 2 to 3 minutes until their flavours are released. Keep moving the spices around to prevent burning.

· Allow the whole spices to cool, then add the cinnamon, and turmeric and mix well.

· Store in a tightly sealed glass jar and use in walnut and pomegranate sauce and other recipes. The seasoning will last for up to 12 months.

I don't always remember where recipes in my collection come from, but I think this one was courtesy of a friend called Josie in Harlow who I did a lot of African food for in another life.

It makes a wonderful gift placed in a pretty glass jar and given with instructions on how to prepare and what to use it in.

Green Banana/Plantain Curry

Green Banana/Plantain Curry

Serves 4-6 | Prep time 4-8 minutes | Cook time 30 minutes

Ingredients

3 tablespoons oil

2 medium onions, finely chopped

1-inch piece of ginger, peeled and grated

4 cloves garlic, peeled and crushed

2-3 teaspoons Maggie's Jamaica Curry Spice

450g green bananas/plantains, peeled and cut into chunks

1 x (400ml) tin coconut milk

1 tablespoon soy sauce

Method

· Fry the onion, garlic and ginger in the oil over medium heat until the onions are transparent, 3-4 minutes.

· Add the Jamaica curry spice and stir-fry for 3 minutes.

· Stir in the green plantains/bananas, coconut milk and soy sauce with enough water to cover.

· Bring to the boil, turn down the heat and simmer for 15-20 minutes, stirring occasionally, until the plantains are tender but not mushy. You may need to add a bit more water as necessary to prevent burning.

I prefer using green plantains in this recipe for a more savoury curry. If green bananas are used, they should be very green and will give the dish a bit of a sweet flavour.

Three Bean and Coconut Curry

Three Bean and Coconut Curry

Serves 4 | Prep time 8-10 minutes | Cook time 35 minutes

Ingredients

350g mixed beans or chickpeas (cooked)

2 tablespoons vegetable oil

1 clove garlic, finely chopped

1 medium onion, finely chopped or blended

10g turmeric

Pinch all spice

1 x (400ml) tin coconut milk

1 teaspoon sugar (optional)

1 teaspoon salt (or according to taste)

1 teaspoon Maggie's Original Hot Sauce (or more if desired)

200-300ml water

Method

· Heat the oil in a saucepan, then add the chopped onions and garlic and stir-fry for 3-4 minutes.

· Add the cooked beans, coconut milk, half the water, turmeric, all spice, sugar (if using), hot sauce and salt according to your taste.

· Allow the contents of the pan to come to the boil with the heat turned up high, then reduce the heat and allow the mix to simmer for 30 minutes – this will allow the flavours to develop and the curry to thicken.

This is my version of a Tanzanian bean stew. It is quick and simple to make and full of goodness – any mixture of beans and pulses can be used.

- Stir from time to time to avoid burning and add more water as needed to prevent the curry drying out.

- Add salt and more chilli if desired, then serve hot with boiled Malawi Kilombero rice or with cornmeal dumplings/polenta.

Tinned chickpeas can be used and the drained liquid saved for the plantain loaf. Chickpea liquid freezes well, but defrost thoroughly before using in other recipes.

Pan-Fried Cauliflower with Ginger and Coriander

Pan-Fried Cauliflower with Ginger and Coriander

Serves 4 | Prep time 6 minutes | Cook time 50 minutes

Ingredients

6 x 2.5cm pieces fresh ginger (peeled and chopped)

1 large cauliflower

8 tablespoons vegetable oil

½ tablespoon ground turmeric

1 fresh hot green chilli

1 bunch fresh coriander leaves, coarsely chopped

1 teaspoon ground cumin

2 teaspoons ground coriander

1 teaspoon Jamaican curry spice

1 tablespoon lemon juice

Salt to taste

Method

· Make ginger paste with 4 tablespoons of water and the peeled, chopped ginger.

· Break the cauliflower into small florets, washing and draining them in a colander.

· In a large saucepan, heat the oil over a medium heat, add the ginger paste and turmeric and stir-fry for 2 minutes.

I was inspired by a vegan customer to try my spices with pan-fried cauliflower, and that suggestion inspired me to modify a recipe I usually taught in my world cookery classes to give it that African flavour.

- Add the green chilli and fresh coriander and cook for another 2 minutes.

- Add the cauliflower and cook for 5 minutes, stirring often. To prevent burning, add 1 teaspoon of warm water as required.

- Add the cumin, coriander and curry powder (or use Naija This & That Seasoning), lemon juice, salt and 3 tablespoons of water then stir-fry for 3-4 minutes. Cover the pan and simmer for 35-40 minutes, stirring occasionally. The cauliflower is ready when tender with just a trace of crispiness along its inner spine.

Stir-Fried Broccoli

Stir-Fried Broccoli

Serves 4 | Prep time 5 minutes | Cook time 5 minutes

Ingredients

450g broccoli

1½ tablespoons groundnut oil

2 tablespoons garlic, coarsely chopped

1 teaspoon salt

½ teaspoon ground black pepper

2 tablespoons of dry sherry

1 tablespoon Maggie's Roasted Chilli with Balsamic Sauce

1 teaspoon sugar

4-5 tablespoons water

2 teaspoons sesame oil

Method

· Separate the broccoli heads into small florets and peel and slice the stems.

· Blanch the broccoli pieces in a large pan of boiling water until just tender, then immerse in cold water. Drain thoroughly.

· Heat a wok or large frying pan over a high heat until hot. Add the oil, when it is very hot and slightly smoking, add the garlic, salt pepper, sherry, Maggie's roasted chilli with balsamic sauce and sugar. Stir-fry for a few seconds.

· Add the blanched broccoli and water.

· Stir-fry over a moderate to high heat for 4 minutes until the broccoli is heated through.

· Garnish with the sesame oil and continue to stir-fry for 30 seconds.

· The broccoli is now ready to serve.

At one point in my cooking journey I taught cooking for pleasure, covering dishes from Japan, Asia, India and other countries, and this recipe is a happy nod to my Chinese cooking classes.

Sweet Potato with Peanut Butter Stew

All over the African continent there is a recipe using groundnuts, or peanuts, in cooking, from as simple as roasted and boiled groundnuts to substantial stews that can be served with rice, eba dumplings or other variations of dumplings.

Sweet Potato with Peanut Butter Stew

Serves 6 | Prep time 8-10 minutes | Cook time 45 minutes

Ingredients

800g sweet potatoes, peeled and cut into chunks

400g salad tomatoes, chopped

3 tablespoons vegetable oil

2 medium onions, 1 roughly chopped and 1 finely chopped

8 cloves garlic, crushed

1 teaspoon cinnamon powder

½ teaspoon ginger powder

½ teaspoon ground cloves

1 tablespoon Maggie's Chilli Sauce (chilli powder)

400g water or vegan stock

1 bunch coriander, chopped

1 x (400ml) tin coconut milk

300g peanut butter

Salt to taste

Method

· In a large saucepan on high, heat the oil and add the roughly chopped onions, then add the finely chopped onions and stir-fry for a minute.

· Add the crushed garlic and stir-fry for 30 seconds until the onions begin to soften.

· Add the cinnamon, ginger and cloves and mix in well, followed by the sweet potatoes.

In this recipe sweet potato is used to give a certain sweetness that compliments the peanuts. In original recipes groundnuts would be dry roasted then processed for use in the recipe, but peanut butter makes a more readily available alternative and adds a certain creamy texture to the dish.

- Add the chopped tomatoes, peanut butter and chilli sauce and stir until mixed in, about 2-3 minutes.

- Pour in the coconut milk and half the water or stock and bring everything to a boil. Reduce the heat to a simmer and allow the sweet potatoes to cook for about 35 minutes, until they are tender and the stew is thick, stirring occasionally.

- Taste and adjust the seasonings and add more water as required. Stir in the chopped coriander just before serving with steamed Malawi Kilombero rice.

Courgette, Kale and Leek Bitetuteku

Courgette, Kale and Leek Bitetuteku

Serves 4-6 | Prep time 10-12 minutes | Cook time 13-18 minutes

Ingredients

200g kale

1 courgette, diced

1 small leek, chopped

1 garlic clove, crushed

1 teaspoon Maggie's Ultimate Veg Spice (or any favourite spice)

2 teaspoons tomato puree

1 tablespoon palm or olive oil

Salt and guinea pepper to taste

Method

· Heat the palm or olive oil and stir-fry the onions, leeks and garlic for 3-5 minutes.

· Add the kale and mix in.

· Add the tomato puree and Ultimate Veg Spice and simmer for 8-10 minutes until the kale is wilted. To prevent burning, add a tablespoon of water at this point if required.

· Add the diced courgettes and heat through for 2-3 minutes.

· Season with salt and guinea pepper and serve.

Leeks are such a big part of Welsh food when they are in season. I was excited to come across this recipe when researching for one of my pop-up African evenings and just had to include it here. It is also another way to use the increasingly popular kale. Try cavolo nero or black kale when available for a nice variation.

Green Bean Casserole

Green Bean Casserole

Serves 8 | Cook time 20-45 minutes

Ingredients

600g frozen French-cut green beans

1 x (400g) can cream of mushroom soup (or make your own)

100g fried onion rings

1-2 teaspoons Maggie's Green Chilli Sauce

Method

· Place the beans, soup and fried onions in an ovenproof casserole dish with a touch of the Maggie's Green Chilli Sauce.

· Put the casserole dish in the oven at 180°C for 20 minutes. (These will be fine in the oven up for to an hour, they just get more soupy. The casserole can also be cooked in a saucepan for 45 minutes to 1 hour.)

I tend to cut the green beans in half if I am unable to find cut green beans, but that is my preference.

I first experienced this recipe in the USA and quickly added it to my repertoire because of how simple it is to prepare and how easily it can be scaled up to feed a crowd. I could not resist finely chopping up some chillies and adding them to my initial batch.

Desserts

Banfora: Burkina Welsh Cakes

Banfora: Burkina Welsh Cakes

Makes 10-12 | Prep time 10 minutes | Cook time 10 minutes

Ingredients

225g self-raising flour

100g vegan margarine

100g sugar

Pinch salt

50g dried pineapple pieces

2-3 tablespoons soy or other plant-based milk

1 teaspoon mixed spice

Method

· Place the self-raising flour, sugar, mixed spice and pinch of salt into a bowl.

· Rub the margarine into the flour mix with your fingertips until well combined and resembling breadcrumbs.

· Mix in the dried pineapple pieces with a little of the milk until a soft but firm dough is obtained.

· On a lightly floured surface, roll out the dough to about half an inch thickness.

· Cut out rounds using your favourite cookie cutter. Re-roll any leftover dough and repeat the process until all the mix is used up.

· Cook the Burkina cakes on a hot griddle for about 2-3 minutes each side until they are golden brown and cooked through.

· Allow to cool, sprinkle with sugar and serve with tea or a favourite drink.

My first thought when researching the cooking of banfora was, which came first, the Welsh or the Burkina Faso version? Did we swap the raisins or the pineapple pieces? Is this worthy of a research project?

Rum Caramel Oranges

Rum Caramel Oranges

Serves 8 | Prep time 8 minutes | Cook time 35 minutes

Ingredients

225g granulated sugar

2 teaspoons rum

8 small oranges

300ml orange juice

1 teaspoon ground allspice

150ml water

150ml hot water

Method

· Prepare the caramel by placing the sugar in a heavy-based saucepan and adding 150ml of water.

· Heat gently over low heat until all the sugar is dissolved.

· Turn up the heat and boil rapidly without stirring until the mix turns to a rich, golden brown caramel.

· Remove from the heat and add 150ml of hot water, then add the orange juice and rum and the ground allspice. Set aside for the caramel to cool.

· Remove strips of peel from one orange using a potato peeler and cut into thin strips. Set aside.

· Remove the skin and pith from all the oranges using a sharp knife.

· Cut the oranges horizontally into slices, around 6mm thick. Reform the oranges to their original shape and secure with a cocktail stick.

Dessert is a fairly recent concept after meals in West and East African dining. The most common after-dinner serving would be fruit of some sort, or kola/bitter kola nuts. This fruit offering has a touch of tropical sunshine and warmth in the form of rum.

- Place the oranges in a serving bowl and pour over three-quarters of the caramel.

- Place the strips of orange peel in the remaining caramel and cook over low heat for 2-3 minutes.

- Pour over the oranges just before serving.

Chin Chin

I recently made a batch at home and stored it in what I considered a hidden location. When I went to retrieve the chin chin a week later, the cupboard was bare! There are several ways to make chin chin, but here is a vegan alternative that will produce the moreish Nigerian snack.

Chin Chin

Serves 1 | Prep time 10 minutes | Cook time 20-30 minutes

Ingredients

250g plain flour

125g caster sugar

5ml ground nutmeg

50g vegan margarine

60ml chickpea water, whisked to a soft foam

60-80ml extra water or plant-based milk if needed

Vegetable oil for deep frying

Method

· Put the flour and nutmeg into a large bowl.

· Add the margarine and rub into the flour with your fingertips until it looks like fine bread crumbs or use a food processor for 1 minute, set aside.

· In another bowl beat or whisk the chickpea water for 3 to 4 minutes until it becomes a soft foam.

· Add the sugar to the mix and then stir in the chickpea foam and half of the water/milk a bit at a time until a smooth but stiff dough is achieved.

· Next place the dough on a lightly floured surface and knead for 5 to 7 minutes until a smooth but firm dough is achieved (this can be done much quicker in a food processor).

· Using a rolling pin, roll the dough flat to about 1cm thickness, then, with the aid of a pizza wheel or a sharp knife, make even horizontal lines through the dough, then make vertical lines to create little square or diamond shapes. Note that the dough doubles in size when placed in the hot oil, so don't make the pieces too big.

· Add a generous amount of vegetable oil to a deep frying pan and heat until the oil is very hot (160°C if using a fryer).

· Fry the chin chin pieces in small batches making sure not to overcrowd them, stirring continuously, until all the chin chin changes to a light golden-brown colour. If overcrowded the chin chin pieces tend to soak up oil and the resulting batch will be unsatisfactory.

For the chickpea water, open a can of chickpeas and use the liquid; alternatively, reserve the water when you use chickpeas in other recipes. Chickpea water freezes well and needs to be defrosted and brought to room temperature for use in this recipe.

This version produced a less crunchy, lighter variety to the traditional chin chin, but is most satisfying.

Chin chin is a street food and party snack, a favourite at Christmas and Ramadan celebrations.

Clementines in Port

Clementines in Port

Serves 4-8 | Prep time 6-8 minutes | Cook time 13-15 minutes

Ingredients

150ml port/brown rum

100g sugar

1 lemon, rind only

1 stick cinnamon

8 clementines (pears or figs are other options)

Method

· Peel the rind from the lemon and place it in a saucepan with the port/brown rum, sugar and cinnamon.

· Heat gently until the sugar dissolves. Bring to the boil for 3 minutes.

· Carefully peel the clementines, keeping them whole.

· Add to the port syrup and poach gently for about 6-8 minutes until tender.

· Transfer the clementines to a serving dish.

· Remove the lemon rind and cinnamon from the syrup.

· Boil the syrup until reduced by half and pour over the clementines.

· Serve cold with vegan cream if desired.

I grew up with clementines but always called them tangerines and was very surprised to discover that they came in orange colours, as I had only ever experienced them in shades of green. Plentiful at Christmastime, this is a great way to mix your festive alcohol with fruit.

Plantain Loaf

The first time I ate a yummy large macaroon from a vegan stall and was informed there was not an egg in sight, I was inspired to create this version of our popular and tasty plantain loaf. Plantain is a veg that looks like a large banana when ripe, however, it can't be eaten raw nor peeled like a banana. Called dodo in Nigeria, it is a favourite when sliced and fried, but here we present to you a light, succulent loaf with a bit of a Ghanaian twist. In Ghanaian cooking, garlic, ginger and chilli are added to plantain slices before frying to create the dish called kelewele.

Plantain Loaf

Makes 2 loafs | Prep time 15 minutes | Cook time 45-60 minutes

Ingredients

570g self-raising flour

1 teaspoon bicarbonate of soda

650g very ripe (overripe) plantains, peeled and sliced

1 x (400g) tin chickpeas (drained water only)

500g sugar

1 teaspoon ginger powder

1 teaspoon salt

1-2 teaspoons Maggie's Original or Roasted Chilli Sauce

225ml vegetable oil

Method

· Use a food processor with the cutting blade attachment. Grease and line two loaf tins with greaseproof paper.

· Add the self-raising flour, bicarbonate of soda, peeled and sliced plantains, sugar, ginger powder, salt, chilli sauce and vegetable oil to the bowl of the food processor.

· Mix on medium speed for 3-4 minutes until combined. Set aside.

· In a large bowl, whisk the chickpea water on high speed until it forms soft, foamy peaks.

· Add the plantain mix to the whisked chickpea water and stir in gently until well combined.

· Add the mix to the two greased and lined loaf tins (or any other cake tin), place in a preheated oven or fan oven and cook at 180°C for 45 minutes.

- Check if they are cooked through by pushing a slim knife right through the centre – it should come out dry (without any cake mix).

- Allow to stand for 5 minutes, then turn out onto a cooling tray, serving when you are ready.

Puff-puff with Kombucha

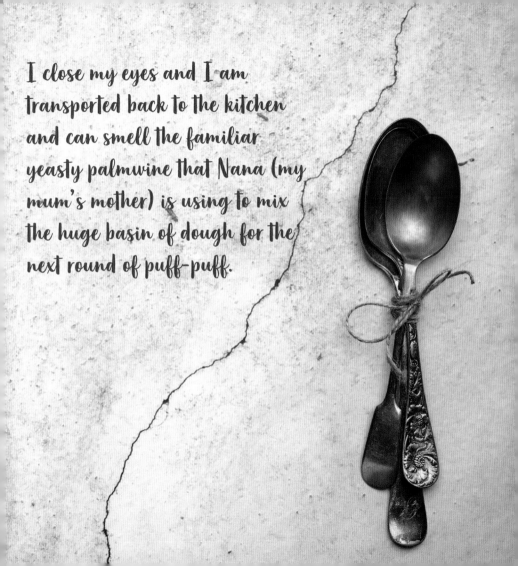

I close my eyes and I am transported back to the kitchen and can smell the familiar yeasty palmwine that Nana (my mum's mother) is using to mix the huge basin of dough for the next round of puff-puff.

Puff-puff with Kombucha

Serves 4 | Prep time 5 minutes (and overnight to rise) | Cook time 20-25 minutes

Ingredients

450ml local cider (the best thing I have found is Blighty Booch Kombucha, rose and nettle flavour, where you can get it)

½ sachet instant yeast

100g sugar (or according to taste)

Pinch ground nutmeg

500g plain flour

Method

· Mix all the ingredients together in a large bowl for a few minutes until properly combined, about 5 minutes.

· Cover tightly with a damp cloth but allow room to expand (cling film will work).

· Set aside in a warm place until doubled in size, or preferably overnight (smell the lovely aroma).

· Heat oil in a deep pan or deep fat fryer. When hot enough, put a tablespoon of the mixture into the oil – do not overcrowd the pan.

· Fry the puff-puff on one side until lightly browned, then flip over and fry on the other side.

· Drain and serve with a sprinkling of sugar if desired and watch it speed off the plate. I have been known to serve this with warm Maggie's Chilli Chocolate Sauce.

I remember how Nana would mix the flour with fresh yeast/fermenting palmwine and then add other ingredients to make her own unique blend of puff-puff. As all the mixing was done by hand, a particular movement was needed.
Even today puff-puff is served as street food in Nigeria, but Nana made the best.

Tips: The oil is hot enough when a small piece of bread begins to sizzle immediately when dropped in. If the oil gets too hot and the puff-puff is browning but not getting cooked in the middle, turn down the heat to medium but not low, as the puff-puff will then absorb too much oil.

Party

Favourites

Ginger is commonly found in African markets and there are several variations of grandma's recipe for a zinging ginger drink.

Ginger Spritzer with Pineapple

Serves 4 | Prep time 15 minutes

Ingredients

1L sparkling water

100g peeled ginger
(frozen can be used)

300g pineapple

5 tablespoons lemon
juice

1½ cups sugar

Method

· Crush the ginger and pineapple.

· Add the sparkling water and lemon juice and then
pass through a sieve.

· Add the sugar and stir until dissolved.

· Refrigerate and serve chilled with a wedge of lemon
and sprig of mint.

Here I have combined my preference for
sparkling water with pineapple, which
is very prolific when in season, to make
a quick, refreshing drink for summer
or winter. Try it warm.

Chickpea Dip

Chickpea Dip

Enough to serve a small party | Prep time 5-6 minutes

Ingredients

1 x (400g) tin chickpeas

1 tablespoon Maggie's Roasted with Balsamic Chilli Sauce

2 cloves garlic

1-2 teaspoons tahini/ sesame paste

1 tablespoon olive oil

1 teaspoon salt, or according to taste

Method

- Place all the ingredients except the olive oil and salt into the jug of a blender/food processor.

- Process on high while drizzling in the olive oil.

- Remove from the jug to a bowl and season to taste with salt and more chilli sauce if required.

- Serve as a side or as part of a vegan platter.

I have been known to use sesame seeds if I run out of sesame paste and it works well.

Don't forget to save the water drained from the chickpeas to use in the plantain loaf or chin chin recipes.

Tomato Dip

Tomato Dip

Serves 4 | Prep time 3 minutes | Cook time 12-15 minutes

Ingredients

75g tomato puree

60ml oil

2 small onions, thinly sliced

2 tomatoes, thinly sliced

1 teaspoon chilli sauce

2 bay leaves

Large pinch nutmeg

Method

· Heat the oil in a firm-based frying pan and stir-fry the thinly sliced onions for 5 minutes.

· Add the tomato puree and keep stir-frying.

· Add the fresh sliced tomatoes, bay leaves, nutmeg, chilli and salt if desired and according to taste.

· Add 150ml of water and bring to the boil. Turn down the heat and allow to simmer until a thick sauce/ dip is achieved. It can be cooled and used as a dip or served hot with fried plantain slices (*dodo*).

Tomatoes are widely used in African cooking and their stews, in their fresh form, as puree or as tinned plum tomatoes. I remember monthly market days with baskets of tomatoes that need to be washed and sorted!

This recipe is inspired by our visit by food to Congo, where we served it as a starter with plain chips.

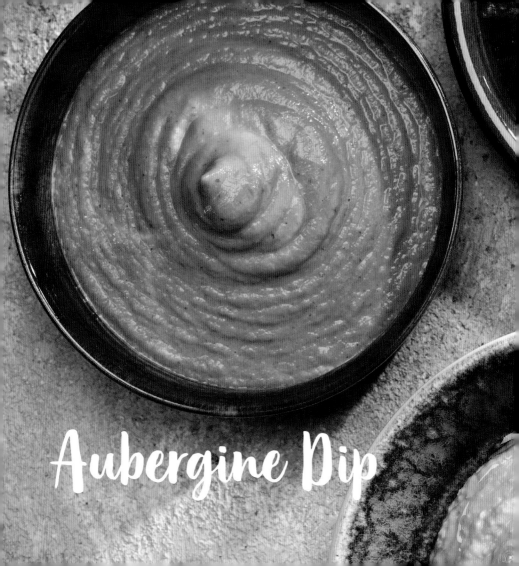

Aubergine Dip

Aubergine Dip

Makes 2 bowls | Prep time 10 minutes | Cook time 25 minutes

Ingredients

2 medium aubergines

2–4 cloves garlic

Pinch salt (or according to taste)

2 tablespoons olive oil

1 teaspoon water

1-2 tablespoons Maggie's Original Chilli Sauce (experiment with the other flavours)

Method

· Wash the aubergines, place them on a baking tray and bake in the oven at 160°C for 30-40 minutes until soft.

· Remove from the oven and allow to cool.

· Place the cooled chopped aubergines into the bowl of a food processor together with the garlic, salt and chilli sauce, cover and process on high, adding a little of the water to help the process if needed.

· Meanwhile, through the opening in the processor lid, drizzle in the olive oil a bit at a time until it is all used up and a smooth, thick paste is achieved.

· Remove from the food processor into a large, clean bowl and adjust the chilli and salt seasonings.

· Serve as a side or as part of a vegan platter. This will last for about 2 to 3 days in the fridge.

Back in 2016, when we first launched the original range of Maggie's Sauces, we looked for different ways to showcase them and get people to try them other than by tasting them directly. So we cut up some carrot and celery sticks, whizzed some baked aubergines in my ever-faithful blender and encouraged the process with a little bit of olive oil. People often asked to buy the aubergine dip, and here is a much worked on version of the original.

Maggie Ogunbanwo

Following on from the international award-winning *The Melting Pot*, Maggie Ogunbanwo, founder, CEO and bottle washer at Maggie's African Twist (www.maggiesafricantwist.com), shares with us her love for food in an African Twist. Everyday recipes and favourites old and new can be given that African twist with a touch of chilli or spice or just Maggie's touch.

Maggie, mother of two and wife to Olufemi, is proud to live and work in North Wales, with her roots in Cameroon and Nigeria, West Africa. She has been experimenting with food since she was old enough to grab a few things from her mother's kitchen and head to the garden for cooking trials.

Maggie's hands were untied in her thirties when she came to realise that her understanding of food is a gift that not everyone is born with. She seeks to showcase this through talks, demos and recipe books, but dearest to Maggie's heart, however, is the need to untie other women's hands so they may live their best lives.
maggiesafricantwist.com

Huw Jones

Huw is a specialist food photographer with over 35 continuous years' experience in producing professional photography for a global client base. His specifically designed studio is the best equipped in the UK, with all dishes prepared and photographed on site using the highest-standard industry equipment.

Huw's stunning images showcase Gilli Davies's recipes in the Graffeg's Flavours of Wales and Flavours of England series, as well as the range of seasonal cookbooks from Angela Gray's Cookery School.

André Moore

Head Chef André Moore was born in Cardiff to a multi-cultural family and brought up in a melting pot of different cultures, foods and flavours. Both his father and stepfather Mike (a keen cook) come from Merchant Navy backgrounds and are responsible for introducing him to a host of new and exciting world ingredients from an early age. Taking this as his inspiration, he extensively travels, picking up new ideas and flavour combinations on the way.

Now with more than 25 years' experience of professional cooking, André splits his time between cooking for the Wales rugby team and working with Huw Jones producing perfectly presented food photography for a list of global clients.

Metric and imperial equivalents

Weights	Solid	Volume	Liquid
15g	½oz	15ml	½ floz
25g	1oz	30ml	1 floz
40g	1½oz	50ml	2 floz
50g	1¾oz	100ml	3½ floz
75g	2¾oz	125ml	4 floz
100g	3½oz	150ml	5 floz (¼ pint)
125g	4½oz	200ml	7 floz
150g	5½oz	250ml	9 floz
175g	6oz	300ml	10 floz (½ pint)
200g	7oz	400ml	14 floz
250g	9oz	450ml	16 floz
300g	10½oz	500ml	18 floz
400g	14oz	600ml	1 pint (20 floz)
500g	1lb 2oz	1 litre	1¾ pints
1kg	2lb 4oz	1.2 litre	2 pints
1.5kg	3lb 5oz	1.5 litre	2¾ pints
2kg	4lb 8oz	2 litres	3½ pints
3kg	6lb 8oz	3 litres	5¼ pints

Acknowlegements

My thanks go first to Peju Ajayi Obe Odjiko, my friend and classmate from years back. She furnished me with ideas and images for a whole month of Veganuary in 2020. I am able to do this work because of you.

My son started me on plant-based milks and since then I have had a dry nose. Anytime I find something that I can modify for vegan palates in my journey by food around the African continent, I think, Toda would like this. Thank you, son.

Thanks go to Caroline Hannah for muting the idea of a vegan cookbook some years back and to the Graffeg and Huw Jones teams for bringing the dream to life.

I hope you enjoy it all.

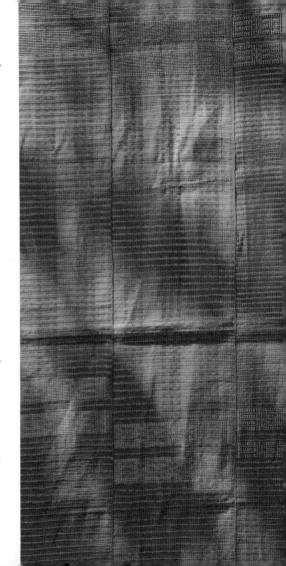

Notes

Notes

Notes

Notes

Notes

Notes

Notes

Notes

Notes

Notes

African Twist
Published in Great Britain in 2022 by Graffeg Limited.

Recipes by Maggie Ogunbanwo copyright © 2022.
Food photography by Huw Jones copyright © 2022.
Food styling by André Moore.
Prop styling and post-production by Matt Braham.
Designed and produced by Graffeg Limited copyright
© 2022.

Graffeg Limited, 24 Stradey Park Business Centre,
Mwrwg Road, Llangennech, Llanelli, Carmarthenshire,
SA14 8YP, Wales, UK. Tel: 01554 824000.
www.graffeg.com.

Maggie Ogunbanwo is hereby identified as the author of
this work in accordance with section 77 of the Copyrights,
Designs and Patents Act 1988.

The publisher acknowledges the financial support of the
Books Council of Wales. www.gwales.com.

ISBN 9781802580754

1 2 3 4 5 6 7 8 9

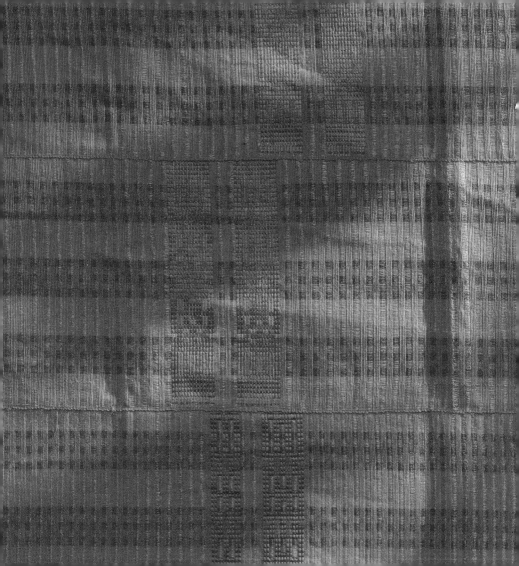